KT-132-286

Write Your Own
History Stories

Tish Farrell

NB 1860 079253 8004

Leabharlanna Atha Cliath
CABRA LIBRARY
Invoice : 07/1789 Price EUR8.75
Title: Write your own histor
Class: J 808·02

Leabharlann na Cabraí
Cabra Library
Tel: 8691414

Your writing quest

Do you have a passion for the past? Would you like to travel back in time: be an Egyptian pyramid builder or a jousting medieval knight? If you long to bring historical events to life in your own stories, this book will show you how to write your own historical fiction. It may not be a time machine, but it's the next best thing.

Your first challenge is to discover your own Long-lost Story Archive – the secret files of imagination that we all have hidden in our minds. Then you must learn some special skills to help you 'travel' back to your chosen time. This book contains plenty of advice and exercises to help you on your way. There will be tips and guidance from famous writers and examples from their books to give you more ideas.

But don't forget! Becoming a good writer takes time and practice. Like all the best quests, there are few shortcuts.

Now get ready to spark up your time machine...

Bon voyage!

Copyright © ticktock Entertainment Ltd 2006
First published in Great Britain in 2006 by ticktock Media Ltd.,
Unit 2, Orchard Business Centre, North Farm Road, Tunbridge Wells, Kent, TN2 3XF
We would like to thank: Starry Dog Books for their help with this book.
ISBN 1 86007 925 3 PB
Printed in China
A CIP catalogue record for this book is available from the British Library.
All rights reserved. No part of this publication may be reproduced, copied, stored in a retrieval system, or transmitted in any form or by any means electronic, mechanical, photocopying, recording or otherwise without prior written permission of the copyright owner.

CONTENTS

WANT TO BE A WRITER?

This book aims to give you the tools to write your own historical fiction. Learn how to craft believable characters, perfect plots, and satisfying beginnings, middles and endings.

Step-by-step instruction

The pages throughout the book include numbers providing step-by-step instructions or a series of options that will help you to master certain parts of the writing process. To create beginnings, middles and ends, for example, complete 20 simple steps.

Chronological progress

You can follow your progress by using the bar located on the bottom of each page. The orange colour tells you how far along the story-writing process you have got. As the blocks are filled out, so your story will be gathering pace...Each section explains a key part of the writing process, teaching you how to get into the mindset of an author and learn all the necessary skills, from plot structure and viewpoints to adding belieavable dialogue, The process ends by looking at the next step - what do you want to do next after your story is finished.

---

28 THE SUPPORTING CAST

❼ The rest of the cast

The best way to show readers what your hero (protagonist) is really like is to have them interacting with other characters. Minor characters can add light and shade, drama and complication to the story. Your heroes will be also judged by the friends they keep. Scenes between hero and friends are a good way to show the reader what he or she is really like as a person.

❽ Character sketches

Charles Dickens' books are a good place to learn about creating memorable minor characters. In *Great Expectations*, Pip describes his bullying sister, Mrs Joe:

> My sister... had such a prevailing redness of skin, that I sometimes used to wonder whether it was possible she washed herself with a nutmeg-grater instead of soap...
>
> Charles Dickens, *Great Expectations*

Case study

Dickens' books are full of larger-than-life characters, but Dickens was also fascinated by ordinary people and their mundane lives. In one of the *Sketches by Boz*, he wrote: 'It is strange with how little notice, good, bad or indifferent, a man may live and die in London. His existence is a matter of interest to no one save himself; he cannot be said to be forgotten when he dies, for no one remembered him when he was alive.'

| GETTING STARTED | WRITING STYLES AND IDEAS | CREATING CHARACTERS | VIEWPOINT |

Box features

Appearing throughout the book, these four different colour-coded box types help you with the writing process by providing inspiration, examples from other books, background details and hints and tips.

TIPS AND TECHNIQUES

Some historical stories feature real-life figures – often kings and queens. But it's safest to have them only as 'walk-on' characters. In A Northern Light, for example, Jennifer Donnelly uses the letters of the real Grace Brown who drowned at Big Moose Lake in July 1906.

Now it's your turn

More character building

For ten minutes, brainstorm a brief biography of one of your minor characters – a protagonist or an antagonist. Say what their role is in your story. Find a few special features that make them stand out – a sense of humour, a limp, bright red hair, etc. Write your first thoughts only.

❾ Reveal character

In Jennifer Donnelly's *A Northern Light*, heroine Mattie and her friend Weaver Smith's love of words shines out in the 'word duels' they play over the word 'iniquitous':

*Evil! Weaver
yelled.
Immoral!
I shouted.
Sinful!
Wrong!
Unrighteous!
Unjust!
Wicked!
Corrupt!...*

Jennifer Donnelly,
A Northern Light

SYNOPSES & PLOTS   WINNING WORDS   SCINTILLATING SPEECH   HINTS & TIPS   FINISHING TOUCHES   WHAT NEXT?

Tips and techniques boxes

These boxes provide writing tips that will help you when you get stuck, or provide added inspiration to get you to the next level.

Now it's your turn boxes

These boxes provide a chance for you to put into practice what you have just been reading about. Simple, useful and fun exercises to help you build your writing skills.

Quote boxes

Turn to these green boxes to find quotes taken from published historical-fiction books by popular authors, from Rosemary Sutcliff to Elaine Marie Alphin.

Case study boxes

These boxes provide history on famous historical-fiction writers - what inspired them, how they started and more details.

WHY DO WRITERS WRITE?

Storytelling of all kinds is a special skill and success will not come overnight. Most well-known writers took years to get published – and few authors make a living from their books. So why do writers write? They write to tell a story that must be told and because they believe that nothing is more important than stories.

Celia Rees

Celia Rees (right), author of *Witch Child*, realised that the skills that condemned a woman to death in 17th-century Europe were valued among Native North Americans (above). What if a girl could move between those two societies? She says:

Writing a book, any book, is like taking a journey. You know the starting point, and (more or less) where you are heading, but you have no way of knowing exactly what is going to happen in between.

Rosemary Sutcliff

Rosemary Sutcliff, author of *Tristan and Iseult*, was born in England but spent her early life in Malta. She wrote 46 novels for young people. She was a sickly child and was home-schooled, and it was during this time that her mother read her the Celtic and Saxon legends that were to fire her love of history.

Elaine Marie Alphin

Elaine Marie Alphin (right in picture), author of *Ghost Soldier*, wanted to be a palaeontologist when she grew up, but writing became her great love. She says: *I write to make sense of my life, and out of the world around me. I write to explore new ideas...*

Karen Cushman

Karen Cushman, author of *Catherine, Called Birdy*, didn't start writing books professionally until she was 50 years old. She especially likes the Middle Ages because big changes were happening in the way people thought about their own identity, and how they looked and behaved, and these have parallels with issues that young people face today. She says:

My ideas come from reading and listening and living; they come from making mistakes and figuring things out. Ideas come from wondering a lot – such as what would happen if...and then what would happen next?

FIRST THINGS FIRST

Historical story writers transport their readers back in time by the power of their words. The first thing you need to do to succeed is gather your writing materials and find a good place to work. All you need is a pen and paper – or quill and ink! – but a computer will make writing quicker.

❶ Gather your writing materials

As a historical-fiction writer you'll need to delve into the past – at your museum and library and on the Internet. To help organise your findings, you may find the following useful:

- A small notebook that you carry everywhere.
- Plenty of scrap paper for writing practice.
- Pencils and pens for drawing ancient maps and timelines.
- Post-it notes to mark reference book pages.
- Stick-on stars for highlighting key information in your research notes.
- Files to keep your fact-finding organised and story ideas safe.

- Index cards for recording key facts.
- Dictionary, thesaurus, encyclopaedia.
- A good general history book to check basic facts.
- A camera to record any historic sites you visit.

❷ Find a writing place

Writers can work where they choose. Some have writing shacks with lots of inspiring objects around them. Some work in bedrooms. Find somewhere comfortable – perhaps your bedroom, the library, or even your local museum. But wherever you choose, sit up straight as you write. Hunched-up work blocks the flow of oxygen to the brain and makes the 'mists of time' seem even mistier.

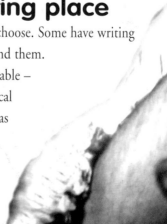

❸ Create a writing zone

- Play music from your favourite historical period.

- Have some historical images laid out around you.

- Put on a hat that you only wear when you're writing (make one or adapt one you already have).

- Try writing with a quill pen and ink!

- Choose intriguing objects for your desk – an old family photograph, a war medal, a shard of ancient pottery, an arrowhead – anything that has a story to tell.

TIPS AND TECHNIQUES

Once you have found your writing place, the golden rule of becoming a real writer is: Go there as often as possible, and write something! This Is calle the wrIters golden rule.

❹ Get in training

Before you can bring the past to life in historical fiction, you must get into training. The best writers practise writing every day, even when they don't feel inspired. So train as you would to be an athlete!

❺ Brainstorming

Thinking about great events in the past can help you come up with ideas. A momentous event such as the 18th-century 'Boston Tea Party', where American colonists rebelled against their British masters, might spark off a series of promising story ideas you could follow up. Think about how many other historical events, phrases and names might help you come up with your own stories. It's a good idea to write down every thought you think, as they might all be useful to you at a later date, and you don't want to risk forgetting an idea that might later turn into a great story.

TIPS AND TECHNIQUES

Come peasants' revolt or the fall of Rome, keep your date with your desk. Don't let anything put you off your writing. Even two minutes' practice a day is better than none and the more you write, the better you will become.

Now it's your turn

A slice of time

Think about your favourite historical event. Imagine a time machine has taken you back there. Close your eyes and try to visualise it. What can you feel, hear, smell, touch and see? Take ten minutes to write down all your first thoughts. Don't worry about complete sentences. Scribble down every impression, even if it seems silly. This is about becoming a writer, not about being the best writer.

❻ Reward yourself!

When you've finished, give yourself a gold star. You have unlocked your Long-lost Story Archive. The more you do this, the easier it will be to overcome the Story Executioner – your internal critic that always finds fault with your writing.

Case study

In 1930, Laura Ingalls Wilder couldn't find a publisher for her autobiography **Pioneer Girl,** *so she used parts of it to create the first of the much-loved Little House books –* **Little House in the Big Woods.** *This story is based on Laura's pioneering life in the big woods of Wisconsin during the late 19th century. Because the writer changed some of the facts, it is called historical fiction rather than autobiography.*

❼ Read, read, read!

Reading lots will help you decide which period you most want to write about, and should spark ideas. Jot them down in a notebook. You should also read outside the historical fiction genre, and pick up classics written in the past by great writers. Mark Twain and Charles Dickens (left) were not historical-fiction writers. They wrote about their own times. But their books may help you 'tune in' to the different ways people thought, talked and lived in the past.

❽ Discover your tastes

Do you enjoy a straightforward historical story like *Witch Child* by Celia Rees? Or how about stories that link modern times with the past, such as *Ghost Soldier* by Elaine Marie Alphin? Would you rather read Kevin Crossley-Holland's accurate picture of 12th-century life, *Arthur – The Seeing Stone*? You might even think about telling a story in pictures like Eric Shanower in *Age of Bronze: A Thousand Ships*.

Now it's your turn

Gaining inspiration

Re-read your favourite historical-fiction novel. Imagine you are writing it. Look at how the writer uses specific historical details to bring the past to life. Make notes on your thoughts. Copy out one or two of your favourite passages. Underline the details that make a scene work. Try to sketch out what you are reading. Ask yourself if you have understood the scene better by drawing it. Did it give you any new ideas about what was happening?

Case study

Joseph Bruchac writes historical novels that show the important place of Native Americans in American history. Much of his writing draws on his Abenaki ancestry. His American Indian heritage is just one part of an ethnic background that includes Slovak and English blood, but it is the element that has shaped his life the most.

❾ Look more deeply

Go back to a favourite historical-fiction story, and as you read, imagine that you are writing it. Start looking for the things that make that world so believable. When you first read it you probably completely lost yourself in it, and forgot all about the real world.

❿ Make reading enjoyable

Grow your imagination. But if you are not enjoying a book, leave it and start another. Make a note of why you didn't like it. You might find this information useful later. Read some non-fiction history books, too.

TIPS AND TECHNIQUES

As you read, think about whose story you want to tell. In which time and place do they live? Record all ideas in your notebook so you will have plenty to draw on for your own story.

A WRITER'S VOICE

Reading lots of good books will help you discover your own writer's voice (your own style of writing). It takes most writers a long time to develop their voice.

) Finding your voice

Once you start reading as a would-be writer, you'll see that writers have their own rhythm and range of language that stays the same throughout the book. Karen Cushman (*Catherine, Called Birdy*) writes quite differently from Harry Mazer (*A Boy At War*), and Kevin Crossley-Holland (*Arthur – The Seeing Stone*) writes nothing like Terry Jones (*The Lady and the Squire*), even though they both write about boys going to war in the Middle Ages.

Experiment

For storytelling ideas, try reading other genres. Caroline Lawrence sets her detective stories in Ancient Rome (below). Legends might inspire you, too, as they did Kevin Crossley-Holland in the *Arthur* series.

TIPS AND TECHNIQUES

As a writer of historical stories, don t be tempted to use old-fashioned language. Readers quickly tire of too many unfamiliar words. Instead, use occasional terms like greetings to suggest a particular time.

WRITERS' VOICES

1665, Derbyshire, England

A parcel of patterns brought the Plague to Eyam. A parcel sent up from London to George Vicars, a journeyman tailor...This was the common report and credence amongst us, though I heard later that the Plague was at Derby at the time when it reached us...

Jill Paton Walsh, *A Parcel of Patterns*

1850s, Mississippi, USA

*Julilly ached with tiredness and hunger gnawed wildly at her stomach...
The other slave girls along the floor slept heavily, but Liza was restless...*

"You is a friend", the crippled girl whispered; "No one else ever picked the high cotton that my poor ol' back won't stretch to."

Barbara Smucker, *Underground to Canada*

Second World War, England

*When Chas awakened, the air-raid shelter was silent. Grey winter light was creeping round the door-curtain. It could have been any time. His mother was gone, and the little brown attaché case with the insurance policies and bottle of brandy for emergencies...
The all-clear must
have gone.*

Robert Westall, *The Machine Gunners*

1192, Welsh Marches, Welsh/English borders

The bodies of the two men were buried in the same pit in the north corner of the churchyard, while their heads were buried in a hole in the south corner.

"And that way," said Oliver, *"their ghosts won't be about to trouble you."*

Kevin Crossley-Holland, *Arthur – The Seeing Stone*

❸ Use what you know

To write historical fiction, you must be a good storyteller and a diligent history sleuth. It may help to start with a period you have studied at school. Look through your past school assignments – maybe the Ancient Egyptians or the Middle Ages. Start looking for your hero. Search for a dilemma. What's happening in their world that is causing them big problems? Ask yourself questions to help find the story.

❹ Do your research

Patricia Curtis Pfitsch says the idea for *Riding the Flume* came from reading a non-fiction book about sequoia trees. The controversial felling of the trees was just the sort of conflict a storyteller needs. Out of her research into the issue grew Francie. This is part of the plot summary from the book's back cover:

During the summer of 1894, the giant sequoia trees – the oldest living things on earth – are being felled for lumber in northern California. Francie finds a note in a hole of an old sequoia stump and recognises her sister's handwriting. But Carrie died in an accident six years earlier. Could the secret still be important? Francie is determined to find out.

Patricia Curtis Pfitsch, *Riding the Flume*

Now it's your turn

Fact to fiction

You are in a plague-ridden city of the mid-1600s. The sick are locked in their houses. Carts collect the dead. Dog catchers round up stray animals. Pretend you are a lost spaniel. How do you survive on the streets? How do you escape the dog catcher? For historical information read Pamela Oldfield's *The Great Plague: The Diary of Alice Paynton*: London 1665–1666.

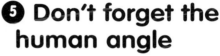

❺ Don't forget the human angle

Historical research gives you details of places, events and human conflicts.

The historical-fiction-writer's art is to shape them into a gripping personal story. For example, in *Riding the Flume,* the main story isn't about felling sequoias. It is about Francie and her reaction to the tree felling. Readers are involved with her dilemmas. They want to know how she will save some of the sequoias, how she will solve the mystery of her dead sister and if she will have the courage to ride the flume. The research helps writers to create a believable and exciting tale.

❻ Ask the family

Many historical-story writers start out by basing their stories on their own family's history. Quiz older family members for their memories. There may be old photo albums, wills, family recipes or letters. This evidence from your own family's past may 'speak' to you in surprising ways.

❼ Is there a problem?

Go back to the exercise you did on page 11, writing down your thoughts about a historical event. Did you have any problems – details you didn't know about dress, transport or the way of life? Perhaps you put in things that hadn't been invented yet – a Japanese car, a skateboard or a computer? This is easily done, so don't worry!

Case study

Mildred D. Taylor (Roll of Thunder, Hear My Cry) was born in Mississippi, the great-granddaughter of a white plantation owner and a slave. She grew up listening to her father's stories about slavery. Years later, when she was trying to tell her grandmother's story about the felling of trees on their family land, the strong-willed character of Cassie Logan emerged, leading to Mildred's books about the Logan family in 1930s' America.

Now it's your turn

Every picture tells a story

Take a break from writing. Capture the past in drawings. Make a scrapbook or collage of everyday life in your chosen historical time. Download images from the Internet or ask the librarian if you can photocopy some pictures from books. Pictures give you something concrete to describe in stories. Visit your museum and draw any relevant objects. If you are allowed to touch them, go for it! Find out what it's like to handle a pistol or turn a butter churn.

❽ Use libraries and museums

Family history is often patchy – people forget things or remember them wrongly. So head for the library and ask the librarian what kinds of historical documents you can consult. For example:

• Old newspapers on microfilm can tell you a lot about the way of life.

• Maps and directories show how your town grew.

• Census schedules record who lived where and how they made a living.

• Copies of wills, deeds and probate inventories list people's possessions.

• Church records and parish registers record births, marriages and deaths.

❾ Be organized

Use index cards to record facts and where you found them. Ring binders with plastic sleeves are good for storing pictures and newspaper cuttings.

❿ Research a setting

In historical stories the setting must be accurate, and it must include the time and the place. Don't overload your story with details, however. It's rather like preparing a stage for a play – just the right props must be there for the actors to act out their parts, but no clutter.

⓫ Draw on your experiences

Think how you feel when you visit another country or an unfamiliar part of your own town. What do you notice most? Is it the shops, the streets or the way people talk, dress or look? Do you notice different food, vehicles or houses? Readers will be interested in the equivalent details from a past time in your story.

Now it's your turn

Start up your time machine!

Imagine you are a tour operator who does guided time-machine trips to your chosen past. Plan your route around your setting. Write a few paragraphs about it. Sketch the tour highlights of your created historical world – maybe a trip up the Nile in a papyrus reed boat, a medicine man's home, a walk along the Great Wall of China or a glimpse of the hangman's noose. Doing this exercise will help you spot gaps in what you know about your own setting.

Case study

*The author Terry Jones created the landscape for his **Saga of Erik the Viking** using his extensive knowledge of the real-life Viking sagas, 12–13th century stories set in Northern Europe. Unfortunately, what he'd found was that they were rather boring. He found the stories quite dry and boring however, so when it came to writing his story he added in extra mystery and adventure to stir the imagination and create "What I'd always hoped the sagas were". Jones always makes sure his stories are historically accurate, from details of battles to information about food and drink.*

⑫ Create the setting

Once you have researched enough facts, creating the setting is rather like doing a jigsaw. Choose only the most vivid, interesting details that affect your characters and plot.

⑬ A location's impact

When you write about the setting of your story, concentrate on details that will dramatically affect your main characters. Is the landscape hazardous to the people in it; does is pose problems for your hero or is it somewhere idyllic?

TIPS AND TECHNIQUES

Put on your characters' skins. Remember! As you go back in time, differences between rich and poor people's lives may be striking. There was far less freedom in every area of life. Values have changed, too. Behaviour that we find shocking now might have been acceptable then, and vice versa.

⑭ Picking details

How will you transport your readers back in time? Think how to bring the past to life in ways that readers can easily relate to. Show what your characters feel; pick out only the most striking things to describe. Think brief. Think sharp. Think exciting. From the start, give them vivid clues to trigger their senses. Have something happening at the same time – something mysterious that snags the readers' curiosity.

⑮ Be authentic

In Jill Paton Walsh's *A Parcel of Patterns*, the simple need to eat (right) shows the historical setting. Eyam villagers are confined to their settlement so they won't spread the plague. Food deliveries to the village boundary chart the plague's course:

> The Duke sent still the bread and bacon and beer to us in ample quantity, soon more by far than the living could eat up. So we took less, and left some lying at the boundary-stones...And the sight of the spare loaves lying struck chill into the hearts of the Duke's servants.
>
> Jill Paton Walsh, *A Parcel of Patterns*

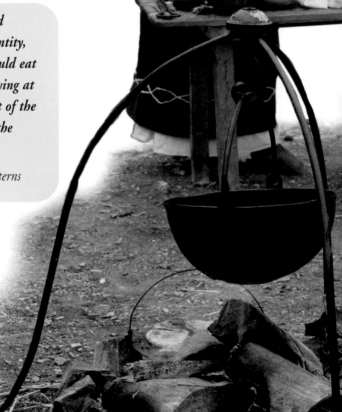

TIPS AND TECHNIQUES

Show historical situations from the main character's viewpoints. Make them personal. Be specific, too: the dead rat stink in the dungeon, roast-hog juices dribbling down a hero's chin.

Now it's your turn

Ace adjectives

Read the quote on page 22 aloud. Notice the verbs and adjectives that really bring the place to life. Then write a scene from your story. Your hero scaling a rampart, pushing through a market, running away.

Use their movement through a specific place to conjure the setting.

⓰ Add action

Mesh the setting with some fast action. In V. A. Richardson's *House of Windjammer*, it is 1636. Hero Adam is dashing through Amsterdam's streets, late for his tutor:

He cut up between the warehouses and into the squeeze of the alleys and streets. Here the streets burrowed between top-heavy houses that sagged under the weight of their upper floors and roofs. At every turn more streets and alleys opened to the left and right, filled with smoke of fires and the belch of pewter factories. Through the maze of sounds and smells... he picked his way until he ran straight into trouble.

V. A. Richardson, *The House of Windjammer*

HEROES

When creating your characters, you must start with the historical facts. Your hero or protagonist will be shaped by the times they live in, just as you are. But to make a good story, they must challenge the system in some way.

❶ Find a hero's name

Names have fashions, so take care. Your Victorian maid won't be called Kylie. Biblical names like Jacob or Job were common in the past. Graveyards and old newspapers are good places to look. Once you have a name, find ways to make your hero sympathetic. If you don't really like them, your readers won't either. This is another reason for giving them some flaws. No one likes a perfect person.

It had to be better than the filthy rooming-house they had left behind in Arkansas, with its rats in the basement and flies in the milk.

Geraldine McCaughrean, *Stop the Train*

❷ Invent a past

Even historical heroes need some history, just enough to explain their current situation. In *Stop the Train*, Geraldine McCaughrean briefly describes pioneer

Now it's your turn

Rough justice?

Brainstorm your feelings. For seven minutes, write about how it felt when you were betrayed, bullied or unfairly accused. Then write for seven minutes from the point of view of the person who hurt you. Well done! You now have some raw materials to help you create your hero's feelings.

Cissie's old life as she thinks of the new one ahead: If your hero has a complicated past, it could be told in a flashback scene, in conversation with a friend or perhaps as a short prologue.

❸ Build a hero

Once you think about your hero's problems, you can start shaping them into a real person. Regard them as a new friend. Ask what they want for a better life. How will they get it? What happens if they fail? Find out their likes and dislikes. What are their strengths and weaknesses? Can these add drama to the story?

❹ Appearance

In real life, people don't often describe themselves directly, so if your hero is your narrator you may have to be cunning. You could get your hero to describe themselves as they look into a mirror, or as they put on clothes for a special occasion. Or perhaps another character can describe them in dialogue.

TIPS AND TECHNIQUES

If you don't know what your hero looks like, search old pictures or photographs. Find a face that fits your story.

❺ What kind of villain?

Heroes need problems to solve. These might be caused by human enemies , by their own flaws, or by war, slavery, plague, invasion or poverty.

❻ Villains as victims

In 16th-century Venice, often only the eldest daughter of a noble household was allowed to marry. If the family was very rich, the second eldest might also. But in Donna Jo Napoli's *Daughter of Venice*, heroine Donata is one of second-born twins:

> *Unless I marry, a convent lies ahead for me, too. I'd die in a convent.*
>
> Donna Jo Napoli, *Daughter of Venice*

TIPS AND TECHNIQUES

Your human villain should be as well thought out as your hero. Don't make them too obvious. They might even start out as your hero's friend.

Enemies everywhere...

Adam Windjammer (*The House of Windjammer* by V.A. Richardson) can't move for enemies, not least the sinister preacher Abner Heems:

> *Abner Heems was just standing there, his hat pulled down low over his eyes...his shoulders hunched against the cold. The preacher had come stealing to their door as quiet as Death.*
>
> V. A. Richardson, *The House of Windjammer*

Picture of cruelty

In Barbara Smucker's *Underground to Canada*, Julilly's main 'enemy' is her life of slavery, but she also has a human enemy – the slave overseer, Sims:

> *Mama Sally held Julilly close as they walked outside and joined the field-hand line. The man with the jay-bird voice strode back and forth in front of them...His cheeks puffed and jiggled as he walked. Julilly noticed that his fingers puffed, too, over the whip that he flicked in his hand.*
>
> Barbara Smucker, *Underground to Canada*

Now it's your turn

Know your villain

Take ten minutes to brainstorm your hero's human enemy. What do they do and what is their motivation? Are they truly bad or simply products of their time? Do they have weaknesses that will affect the story? Say what they look like. Draw pictures, too.

FIRST THINGS FIRST

It is most usual to tell a historical story from your hero's point of view. This makes the story more personal.

❶ The first person

The first-person point of view (POV) speaks directly to the reader, rather like a letter. For example, 'I broke into the castle by swimming the moat' instantly seems more 'real' than 'Squire John broke into the castle.' It gives your story the ring of truth in a way other viewpoints can't. You can use it to tell your story as a narrative, in letters or in diary form. The disadvantage of this POV is that readers only get to know the other characters through the hero's accounts of them, or when they report dialogue.

❷ The third person

The third-person viewpoint (he/she) is where events are described as if viewed from inside your hero's head. Again, readers can only know what other characters are thinking if it is reported in dialogue:

> *Carrie saw the marks of their rubber-soled shoes and felt guilty, though it wasn't her fault. Nick whispered, "She thinks we're poor children, too poor to have slippers," and giggled.*
>
> Nina Bawden, *Carrie's War*

Now it's your turn

A change of view

Write a short scene from your own story. Have your hero doing something with others. Describe the scene as the omniscient narrator (all-seeing view) – saying what is happening to everyone. Then rewrite it in the third person, from your hero's point of view. Finally, try it in the first person. Which version do you prefer and why?

❸ An all-seeing view

Another viewpoint is the omniscient or 'all-seeing' view. It's usually used in traditional stories and it means that readers are told everything the characters think and feel.

❹ Mixed views

In historical stories it is quite common to have diary entries and letters included in the narrative. These give you a chance to change viewpoints in a natural way, for example from third-person narrative to first-person diary or letter extracts.

READY TO WRITE

When your story begins to take shape in your mind, sum up the main theme and plot in a few paragraphs. This is called a synopsis. It will help you keep your story on track. Tell just enough to be intriguing but don't give away the end.

❶ Back cover inspiration

On the back covers of historical novels, the 'blurb' briefly sets the scene and makes readers want to find out more. A synopsis should do the same. Here is an extract from a blurb:

Tom and his friend Ann find life a bit too exciting when they are caught up in the bloodshed and mayhem of the wars between England and France that scarred the 14th century. Tom is kidnapped, falls off a palace, down a well and in love – oh, and he makes a total mess of the Pope's dinner.

Terry Jones, *The Lady and the Squire*

Now it's your turn

Hungry readers

Sum up your story in a single striking sentence, then develop it in two or three short paragraphs. Try to whet your readers' appetites. Show where your story is going without giving away the actual ending.

❷ Create a synopsis

Before they start writing their stories, novelists often list all their chapters outlining what will happen in each one. This is called a chapter synopsis. Once you have worked out the main scenes, you could also develop each one into a separate chapter and so create a novel.

❸ Make a story map

Now you have a synopsis that says what your story is about; a cast of characters; a setting; and you know from whose viewpoint you wish to tell the tale. A useful tool is a story map.

❹ Split into scenes

Before film-makers can start filming, they must know the main story episodes and decide how they can best tell their story in filmed images. To help them, they map out the plot (the sequence of events) in a series of sketches called storyboards. You can do this for your story. Draw the main episodes in pictures. Add a few notes that say what is happening in each scene.

TIPS AND TECHNIQUES

Writing a synopsis can bring unexpected ideas to the surface. If you can't describe your story in a couple of paragraphs, it is too complicated. Simplify it.

❺ Inspiration from a classic

Here are storyboard captions for Robin Hood and Guy of Gisbourne by Howard Pile.

1. It is the time of Richard I, and the Sheriff of Nottingham sends outlaw Guy of Gisbourne, to Sherwood to kill Robin Hood.

2. Robin kills Guy and, disguising himself in Guy's cowl goes to find the Sheriff.

3. Meanwhile, Little John meets a widow whose sons are to be hanged by the Sheriff for poaching.

4. Little John goes in disguise and meets the Sheriff and his prisoners. He agrees to be hangman.

5. Little John frees the brothers but is caught himself.

6. As Little John is to be hanged, Robin arrives, dressed as Guy, and says he has killed Robin.

7. For his reward, he asks permission to kill Little John and has him tied to a tree.

8. Robin frees Little John and tells him to pick up the weapons he has hidden in the wood.

9. Robin reveals who he is, and draws his bow on the Sheriff.

10. The terrified Sheriff and his men flee for the safety of Nottingham's city gates.

❻ Decide to write a novel?

Novels have beginnings, middles and ends just like short stories, but the stories themselves are more complex. They have more details, more character development, and probably several subplots too. In a larger tale, chapters make the storytelling more manageable. Each one has a beginning, middle and end, like a mini-story inside the larger one, but it also carries the story forward, adding more mystery and creating more and more suspense.

❼ Or a short story...

To make the Robin Hood story into a short novel, you would need to think how each storyboard scene could be expanded to show readers more about the characters, their problems and the times they lived in. For example, Chapter 1 might start with some historical scene-setting that demonstrates how the Sheriff of Nottingham has gained so much power. If you include a scene with the Sheriff plotting with Guy, this will show readers what villains they are, and explain their different reasons for wanting Robin dead. A novel, then, is not a short story made longer, but a short story made fatter.

TIPS AND TECHNIQUES

Don't let a novel's length put you off. It's often easier to write a novel than it is to write a good short story.

Now it's your turn

In a circle

If you are struggling with your story map, try this exercise.

1. Sketch your hero in a circle at the centre of a piece of paper. As you draw, imagine that you are that hero, deciding which way to go. Think about the problems they have and what they might do about them.

2. Draw six spokes around your hero circle. Each leads to another circle. Inside each one, sketch a different scene or write it as notes. Each circle will be a course of action that your hero might take, or some obstacle in his or her path.

Give yourself 20 minutes and write down only your first thoughts.

❽ Great beginnings

You have planned your plot and are ready to start your story. Focus on your hero. Put on your hero's skin. Become your hero. Think about 'your' problems. What is at stake? Where will you start the story?

❾ Hook your readers

Some stories leap straight into a dramatic scene, then backtrack shortly afterwards to explain things to readers. Others start with a prologue, giving the historical context. You could start with a brief scene set just before a crisis comes. This lets you show the hero's usual life just before a conflict makes it worse (the Viking invasions, for example). Your hero must then take action or face the consequences.

❿ Bizarre beginnings

In *The Lady and the Squire*, Terry Jones uses some most unexpected comparisons to help us sympathise with hero Tom. The writer speaks directly to the reader about the characters:

> *If you've ever sat astride a man-eating shark and dangled bits of raw flesh in front of it as the creature starts to plunge down into the dark abyss of the sea, taking you with it, you'll have a pretty good idea of how Tom felt in his new job as squire to Henry, Duke of Lancaster. For the time being, Tom was keeping his head above water, but he knew that, at any moment, the Duke might eat him for lunch.*
>
> Terry Jones, *The Lady and the Squire*

⑪ Tense starts

V. A. Richardson's *The House of Windjammer* starts with a shipwreck and the loss of a family fortune. From the first lines, we know things will only get worse for the family:

> *They were lost. All aboard the Sirius knew it now. Lucien Windjammer cursed under his breath. The Sirius rode uneasily on the swell, moving through the fog like a ghost ship.*
>
> V. A. Richardson,
> *The House of Windjammer*

TIPS AND TECHNIQUES

Study lots of opening sentences. Decide which ones work best and why. Make your own opening mysterious or dramatic or funny. Write it and rewrite it. Introduce the conflict at once, or soon afterwards. Send your heroes on their way.

⑫ Increase the tension

Stories often falter after an exciting opening, so be sure to add interest and complication. It is important to find ways to crank up the tension.

⑬ One story inside another

In *The Lady and the Squire*, by Terry Jones, Squire Tom never reaches the end of one quest before another one starts. First Tom is kidnapped and taken to the enemy's torture chamber. Before we find out why, he escapes. He means to return to his own army, but on the way he meets Lady Emily, falls in love, and finds himself rescuing her instead. But before he can do that, he is captured again, falls down a well, and is forced to go on a mission to meet the Pope…Only at the end does all become clear.

⑭ False happy endings

These can be useful part way through a story. In *Catherine, Called Birdy*, by Karen Cushman, Birdy's father decides to marry her off to restore the family fortunes. There is a false happy ending when the heroine succeeds in driving away the first suitor. But then her father comes up with another – maintaining reader interest and building tension.

⑮ Maintain the action

Keep your characters active at all times – battles, chases, runaway horses, shipwrecks, etc. But be sure the action arises from your characters' plans, and not your need to add

TIPS AND TECHNIQUES

If story middles seem 'thin', pile on the challenges for your hero; make their lives a real misery! If you run out of ideas, look through your research notes.

excitement. See how Squire Tom, disguised as a lady's maid, escapes the Archbishop of Reims by doing a handstand:

Gasps came up from the crowd like the air from a dozen blacksmith's bellows. The bull-headed landlord gasped. A dozen servants and a dozen chambermaids gasped.
The Archbishop himself gasped. They all gasped.

At which point, the lady's maid jumped back on her feet, jammed her wimple back on her head, snatched up a large bundle and swept out of the hall.

Terry Jones, *The Lady and the Squire*

⑯ Creating character conflict

Supporting characters can add intrigue and suspense. In V. A. Richardson's *The House of Windjammer*, Jade tries to help Adam. However, because she is his enemy's daughter, Adam suspects her at every turn. This puts both of them in danger.

⑰ Explore weaknesses

Your hero's weaknesses can add real suspense to a tough situation. Peter Gannet in Leon Garfield's *The Empty Sleeve* lets his ambition lead him into dangerous situations. He soon learns that keys are valuable items and can earn him the money he needs to buy his ship's passage. But will his employer find out?

For an alarming instant, as he fumbled for the key behind the mirror, he was glared at by his own reflection; and was shocked by how young and frightened he looked. Shakily he got hold of the key and crept down the stairs with it.

Leon Garfield, *The Empty Sleeve*

⑱ Dramatic climaxes

Stories build in suspense until they reach a climax. After this, the hero's main problems will be solved. If they go back to their old lives, they will have learned something, conquered an enemy or overcome a weakness. In an action story, the climax is likely to be some kind of battle with the main enemy. The enemy might be a person or it might be the learning of a painful truth that sets the hero on a new course and ends the story on a hopeful note.

⑲ New beginnings

Most readers like happy endings of some sort, but don't be predictable. In historical fiction, a typical fairytale ending won't be believable. Instead, focus on what the hero has gained from his or her experience. The hero may have been hurt, but now has a chance to do better and have a good life. Terry Jones' ending to *The Lady and the Squire* suggests more adventures for Tom in the future.

> *Tom shut his eyes, and when he opened them again, the sun had just poked its head above the horizon.*
> *The new day had begun. New adventures lay in store. But which way Tom would go was anybody's guess.*
>
> Terry Jones,
> *The Lady and the Squire*

Now it's your turn

Choose your own ending

Read the ending of your favourite historical fiction. Decide what you liked about it and what you didn't. Write your own ending. Put it aside and read it later. Do you still think your ending is better?

⑳ Painful lessons

Heroes may pay a price for winning in the end. They could lose a friend, a cherished hope or a valued possession. At the very least, they will be older and wiser.

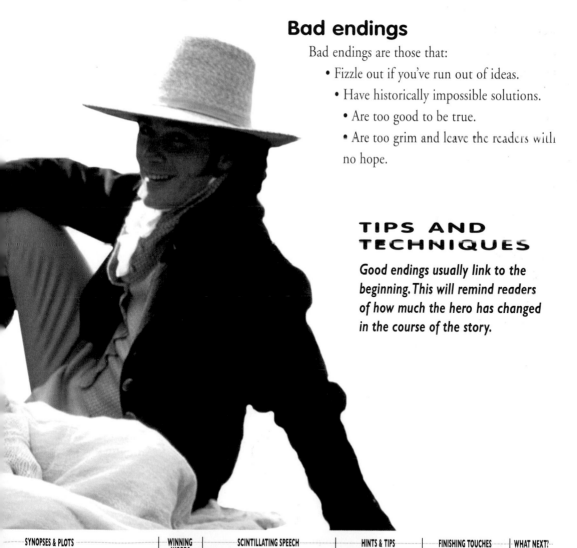

Bad endings

Bad endings are those that:

- Fizzle out if you've run out of ideas.
- Have historically impossible solutions.
- Are too good to be true.
- Are too grim and leave the readers with no hope.

TIPS AND TECHNIQUES

Good endings usually link to the beginning. This will remind readers of how much the hero has changed in the course of the story.

MAKING WORDS WORK

In historical stories, every word must work hard to transport readers back in time. Pick the most telling details to bring the past to life.

❶ Use sharp focus

Choose a few, precise details to create a scene. See how Geraldine McCaughrean describes pioneers stepping off the train in *Stop the Train*:

> *There was a middle-aged man in overalls and a woman's broad-brimmed straw hat...There was a widow in black, with a net purse swinging from her wrist, a knitting bag and a goat.*
>
> Geraldine McCaughrean, *Stop the Train*

❷ Choose words carefully

Use powerful verbs. Sunlight may 'reflect' off a drawn sword. But if it 'glances' this could suggest the blade slashing in battle.

Now it's your turn

Wise words

Pick a word from a favourite book and, with a friend, take turns to see how many words of a similar meaning you can come up with. Or, pick a new word from the dictionary every day. Find ways to use it – make a poem or limerick.

❸ Use vivid imagery

In *The Empty Sleeve*, Leon Garfield uses striking similes a snowstorm is 'like a madman made of feathers' and 'church steeples were as stiff and white as dead men's fingers'. These images foreshadow bad things to come.

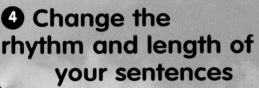

❹ Change the rhythm and length of your sentences

Use short, punchy sentences when describing specific actions. If something scary is going to happen, use longer sentences to build suspense. Here is Peter Gannet being haunted by the whisperings of ghostly apprentices, and that's only the start:

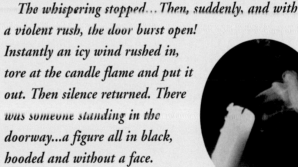

The whispering stopped…Then, suddenly, and with a violent rush, the door burst open! Instantly an icy wind rushed in, tore at the candle flame and put it out. Then silence returned. There was someone standing in the doorway…a figure all in black, hooded and without a face.

Leon Garfield, *The Empty Sleeve*

❺ Change the mood

Serious stories need lighter moments to make difficult scenes bearable, or to distract readers before something really nasty happens. Humorous stories, too, need dashes of drama and pathos to hold readers' interest.

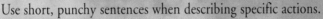

CREATING DIALOGUE

Creating good dialogue is one of the biggest challenges for the historical-story writer. When it's right, it can add colour, pace, mood and suspense to your story.

Let your characters speak

Readers do not want to struggle with writers' attempts at Tudor or medieval dialogue. When in doubt, opt for plain English that omits current expressions. In Karen Cushman's *Catherine, Called Birdy*, the author uses authentic phrases like 'corpus bones' and 'ale head'. But overall the diary is written in understandable English.

❷ Study other historical fiction writers

People often spoke more formally in the past, and people of a lower class would have spoken respectfully to the upper classes. Listen to dialogue in historical TV dramas (right). Old letters can also give us a real sense of the past.

❸ Fictional eavesdropping

Listening to how people around you speak will show you how information flows back and forth between speakers. Notice that people often start mid-sentence or break off without finishing one.

Now it's your turn

Family chat

Spend ten minutes writing down how your family talks at home. Include all the hesitations and repetitions. Compare your notes to some dialogue in a book. You will see at once that it does not include all the hesitations of natural speech. Fictional dialogue gives an edited impression of real speech.

❹ Following convention

The way dialogue is written follows certain 'conventions' or rules. It is usual to start a new paragraph for every new speaker. What they say is enclosed in single or double inverted commas, followed by speech tags ("he/she said", "he exclaimed", "she shrieked") to show who's speaking.

> *"Grandma says your dad ain't got the sticking power of a monkey on a greased pole.'"*
>
> *"Excuse me!" retorted Cissy. "I don't know that someone who ain't acquainted with some other person ought to go bandying monkeys...!"*
>
> Geraldine McCaughrean, *Stop the Train*

⑤ Give information through conversation

If you need to give readers details of a character's actions or history, it's often quicker and more interesting to do it in a conversation. Here's an example from *Carrie's War* (left) by Nina Bawden. Auntie Lou tries to excuse the behaviour of her brother, Mr Evans:

> *"Oh, his bark's worse than his bite. Though he won't stand to be crossed, so don't be too cheeky and mind what he says. I've always minded him – he's so much older, you see."*
>
> Nina Bawden, *Carrie's War*

⑥ Create atmosphere

In Leon Garfield's *The Empty Sleeve*, Mr Bagley, the old ship's carpenter, predicts troubles ahead for the Gannet twins:

> *"I done the best I could for your boys, Mr G.,"* confided the old man, earnestly. *"I rigged their vessels under tops'ls only. That way they'll ride out the squalls...It's best to be prepared for the worst, Mr G., for them squalls has got to come. Most of all, for young Peter here. Saturday's child, born on the chime, will surely see ghosts..."*
>
> Leon Garfield, *The Empty Sleeve*

Now it's your turn

The art of communication

Write a brief, descriptive report on Mr Evans based on Auntie Lou's account of him on page 46. Give some indications of her feelings about her brother. These are only suggested by what she says, but they are quite important. Which version seems more interesting – yours or the original?

❼ Tension through dialogue

Dialogue can be used to create different atmospheres – mysterious, humorous, tragic or happy. It can be used to build tension and foreshadow dangers ahead. In this extract, Adam Windjammer has been waylaid by street boys. Note the sense of menace conjured up by the writer:

"'Looks like a rich boy, Wolfie," one said. "Shut your m-mouth, can't you!" the hungry-looking youth stammered... "How many t times have I told you not to use my name when we're r-robbing?"
"Robbing!" Adam gasped. "But I don't have any money."
"Is that the t-truth of it?" Wolfie said. "Well, we'll be the j-judge of that.'"

V. A. Richardson, *The House of Windjammer*

TIPS AND TECHNIQUES

If any dialogue doesn't advance your story, cut it out.

8 Find different ways of speaking

Good dialogue can reveal what characters are really like. Speech patterns can show social status, education, regional origins and age, as well as suggesting the historical period.

9 Class differences

In *The Empty Sleeve*, Leon Garfield uses modern English, but shows eighteenth-century class differences in the ways characters address one another. Here the young locksmith's apprentice Peter Gannet meets Lord Marriner in the local tavern. The aristocrat calls Peter only by his master's name. In return, Peter speaks deferentially using a formal address, and also rather nervously, as the stammered 'y-yes' hints.

> *"You're Mr Woodcock's boy, aren't you?" said his lordship, kindly.*
> *"Y-yes, your lordship."*
> *The waiter returned with the port.*
> *"Your health, Mr. Woodcock's boy!"*
>
> Leon Garfield, *The Empty Sleeve*

10 Use accents

The extract opposite from *Arthur – The Seeing Stone* shows that Gatty has a country accent. The writer doesn't overdo it, just gives hints with 'why's' and 'I can and all'. In *Underground to Canada*, Barbara Smucker gives the slave girl Julilly a rich turn of phrase that is interesting and easy to follow:

> *"You don't talk nasty like a snake's hiss," she giggled quietly. "Something sure is different about today."*
>
> Barbara Smucker, *Underground to Canada*

⑪ Evoke the past

Caroline Lawrence's *The Roman Mysteries* series has four very different main characters from Roman times: Flavia the aristocrat, Jonathan the outspoken Jewish doctor's son, Nubia a freed African slave who struggles to speak formal Latin, and Lupus a dumb ex street boy. The writer adds occasional words or phrases to suggest the period and the characters' backgrounds.

> "Doctor Mordecai!" gasped Flavia. "You look just like a Roman."
> "Behold!" said Nubia. "You have cut your hairs."
> With his forefinger, Lupus pretended to shave his own smooth cheeks.
> "And shaved off your beard!" agreed Jonathan. "Great Jupiter's eyebrows, father! Why did you do that?"
>
> Caroline Lawrence,
> *The Roman Mysteries*

⑫ Education gap?

Arthur – The Seeing Stone is set in 12th-century England just before the Fourth Crusade. The quest for Jerusalem is on everyone's minds. Here, Gatty, a servant girl, shows her lack of education by asking Arthur, a scholarly lord's son, if Jerusalem is further away than the nearby English city of Chester:

> "'Much, much farther," I said.
> "Why?"
> "Why's because I want to see where Jesus was born. Instead of Ludlow fair, let's go to Jerusalem."
> "Gatty!" I said. "You can't walk to Jerusalem."
> "I can and all," said Gatty.
> "You can't," I said. "Only a magician could. It's across the sea."
> Gatty lowered her head and looked at the ground. "I didn't know that," she said...
>
> Kevin Crossley Holland, *Arthur –
> The Seeing Stone*

Now it's your turn

Who's who?

Choose two characters from historical fiction who are different from each other in a particular way – perhaps one is richer, more educated or from a different place or social class. Invent a conversation between them. Think of ways to show their differences – both in their choice of words and in what they say.

BEATING WRITER'S BLOCK

Sometimes even the keenest writers can run out of words. This is called writer's block. It can last for days (or years!), but regular practice and lots of brainstorming will help. Here are some common causes:

❶ Get over your insecurities

Remember the Story Executioner on page 11 – your internal critic that belittles your work? Well give him the chop.
Do some timed brainstorming at once: the historical figures you'd most like to meet, your time machine's next destinations, how many words mean 'old', etc.

❷ Don't assume other writers are better than you

It is easy to believe that other writers are much better than you will ever be. Even experienced writers fall into this trap. But remember, the more you practise, the more you will improve. You could use your skills to write for history magazines. Documenting the past is the biggest story of all!

Case study

The poet Samuel Taylor Coleridge is one of the first known cases of writer's block. In 1804 he wrote: Yesterday was my Birth Day. So completely has a whole year passed, with scarcely the fruits of a month – O Sorrow and Shame. I have done nothing!

Now it's your turn

Mystery time travel

In your next writing practice, imagine you are travelling in your time machine once more. It stops. The door opens. Step outside. Search for clues that tell you where you've landed. Are you pleased or petrified? Pour out your thoughts for ten minutes.

❸ Find fresh ideas

Thinking you have no ideas is a common block, but as a history lover you will never run short. There are centuries' worth of stories waiting to be told. Visit your local museum or national museum (right) or a favourite historic place. Go out and search for a story.

❹ Coping with criticism

No one enjoys rejection or criticism, but it is an important part of learning to be a writer. If you invite someone to share your stories, be prepared for some negative comments. They may be more useful than flattery. See them as a reason to improve and rewrite your story if it really needs it.

SYNOPSES & PLOTS · · · · · · · · · · · · · · WINNING WORDS · · · · · · · · SCINTILLATING SPEECH · · · · · · · · · · · HINTS & TIPS · · · · · · · FINISHING TOUCHES · · · · · WHAT NEXT!

❺ Understanding writer's block

If you are stuck mid-story, you may not have done enough planning. Do you know what your hero really wants? Ask yourself if your plot has left him or her stranded.

❻ Ask "What if?"

'What if?' is a good question to ask if your story isn't quite clear. What if my hero is really a nobleman's son, but doesn't realise it, like Oliver Twist (right) in Charles' Dickens' book, seemingly condemned to life in the workhouse. What will he do if he finds out.

Interrogate your characters

If you still don't know your hero well enough to work out his or her story, you need to interrogate your character. Think again about what they look like, where they live, what emotions they feel, what they do for a living, what their strengths and weaknesses are, and who their friends and enemies are. To create well-rounded heroes, villains and supporting characters, you need to know these figures yourself inside out.

Keep a Journal

If you keep a journal, you need never stop writing. When you visit museums and other historic places, be sure to record all your thoughts and impressions. These could provide valuable research ideas. Make sure you read what you have written regularly.

❾ Group brainstorming

Writing is a lonely business. If your key character isn't coming to life, brainstorm with friends. Sit in a circle. Start by telling them a brief outline of your character's situation and who they are. Then let everyone ask you questions or make suggestions about what will happen next. It may help you to solve a serious plot problem.

❿ Tell someone else's story

If you really are stuck with your writing, try telling someone else's story. Retell a local legend or use the *Robin Hood* synopsis on page 34 to write your own version of that story. The main thing is to finish it. Completing a piece of storytelling like this will spur you on with your own tales. Prove that you can finish something!

TIPS AND TECHNIQUES

Staring at a blank page, waiting for inspiration to strike, will only give you a headache and make you feel bad about yourself. Brainstorm a list. Write something. 'Something' can always be improved. 'Nothing' can't.

PREPARING YOUR WORK

When your finished story has been 'resting' for a few weeks, it is time to revise and edit it. After the break you will be able to see it with fresh eyes and spot any flaws more easily.

❶ Editing

Reading your work aloud will help you to simplify rambling sentences and correct dialogue that doesn't flow. Underline words that seem weak and replace them with stronger ones – 'dashed' instead of 'went', 'soared' instead of 'flew'. Cut words like 'very' and 'really' and remove unnecessary adjectives. Check your dialogue. Does it sound right? Would an 18th-century housemaid really say 'Whatever!' When your story is as good as it can be, type it up on a computer. This is your manuscript.

❷ Think of a title

A good title is the first thing a reader may notice. It should be intriguing and eye-catching. For ideas, think about some titles that attract you.

❸ Be professional

Manuscripts should always be printed on one side of A4 white paper, with wide margins and double line spacing. Pages should be numbered, and new chapters should start on a new page. At the front, you should have a title page with your name, address, telephone number and email address on it. Repeat this information on the last page.

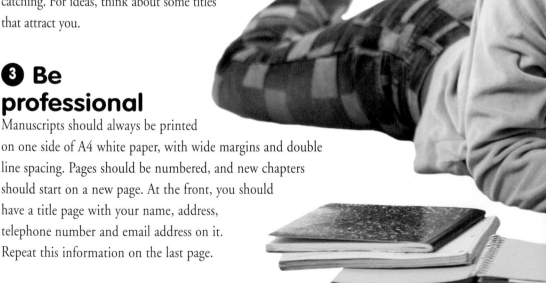

❹ Make your own book

If your school has its own publishing lab, why not use it to 'publish' your own story, or make a class story anthology (collection). A computer will let you choose your own font (print style) and justify the text (making even length margins like a professionally printed page). When you have typed and saved your story to a file, you can edit it quickly with the spell- and grammar checker, or move sections of your story around using the 'cut and paste' facility, which saves a lot of rewriting. Having your story on a computer file also means you can print a copy whenever you need one, or revise the whole story if you want to.

❺ Design a cover

Once your story is in good shape, you can print it out and then use the computer to design the cover. A graphics program will let you scan and print your own artwork, or download readymade graphics. Or you could use your own digital photographs and learn how to manipulate them on screen to produce some highly original images. You can use yourself or friends as 'models' for your story's heroes.

TIPS AND TECHNIQUES

Whether you type up your story on a computer or do it by hand, ALWAYS make a copy before you give it to anyone to read. If they lose it, you lose your only copy!

❻ Some places to publish your story

The next step is to find an audience for your historical-fiction work. Family members or classmates may be receptive. Or you may want to get your work via a publishing house or online site. There are several magazines and a number of writing websites that accept stories and novel chapters from young writers. Some give writing advice. Several run regular competitions. Each site has its own rules about submitting work to them, so make sure you read them carefully before you send in a story. See page 62 for more details. You can also:

• Send stories to your school magazine.
  If your school doesn't have a magazine, start your own with like-minded friends!

• Keep your eyes peeled when reading your local newspaper or magazines. They might be running a writing competition you could enter.

• Check with local museums and colleges. Some run creative-writing workshops during school holidays.

❼ Writing clubs

Starting a writing club or critique group and exchanging stories is a great way of getting your historical-fiction story out there. It will also get you used to criticism from others, which will prove invaluable in learning how to write. Your local library might be kind enough to provide a forum for such a club.

❽ Finding a publisher

Secure any submission with a paperclip and always enclose a short letter (saying what you have sent) and a stamped,

addressed envelope for the story's return. Study the market and find out which publishing houses are most likely to publish historical fiction. Addresses of publishing houses and information about whether they accept submissions can be found in writers' handbooks. Bear in mind that manuscripts that haven't been asked for, or paid for by a publisher – unsolicited submissions – are rarely published.

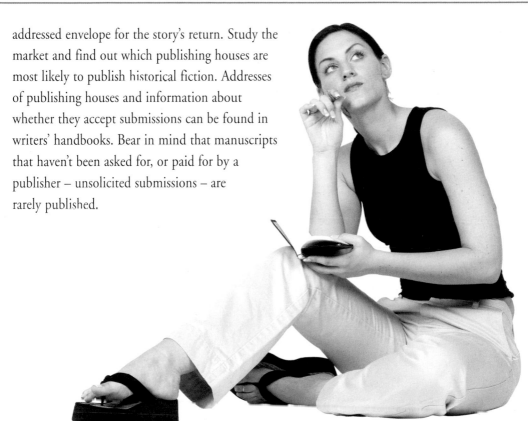

⑩ Writer's tip

If your story is rejected by an editor, don't despair! See it as a chance to make the story better and try again! And remember; having your work published is wonderful, but it is not the only thing. Being able to make up stories is a gift, so why not give yours to someone you love? Read it to a younger brother or sister, or tell it to your grandfather. Your friends are also a ready-made audience.

TIPS AND TECHNIQUES

READ, READ, READ, WRITE, WRITE, WRITE.
It's the only writing tip you will ever need.

WHEN YOU'VE FINISHED YOUR STORY

THE END

Finishing your first story is a wonderful achievement. You have started to master your craft and probably learned a lot about yourself too. Now it's time to start a new tale.

A new angle?

If you did a lot of research for your first story, the chances are you will already have enough material to write another. Perhaps, while you were writing, some other character's story suggested itself? See if there's an angle that demands your attention.

How about a sequel?

Is there more to tell about the characters you have already created? Can you write a sequel that says

what happens next? Celia Rees wrote *Sorceress* as the sequel to *Witch Child*. Perhaps there is a minor character who deserves their own story?

❸ Trilogies

A trilogy usually covers one main story, split over three volumes. V. A. Richardson's *The House of Windjammer* and Kevin Crossley-Holland's *Arthur* books are trilogies. The hero's main problems are revealed in the first book, complicated and expanded in the second and resolved in the third.

❹ Quartets

Joan Lowery Nixon wrote four books in *The Orphan Train Adventures*. The writer was inspired by tragic real-life events in 19th-century America, when poor east-coast families were forced to send their children to the west on the orphan train, hoping they would be adopted by pioneering families who could give them a good life.

❺ Keep researching

Keep looking for stories: visit your museum, look through the history books, learn about a specific invention, read the diary of a real historical figure or nag a grandparent for more family stories.

Joan Lowery Nixon got the idea for her stories this way. She wanted to *bring history and fiction together in an exciting, adventurous time and place, to tell the stories of those who could have travelled west on the orphan train.*

anachronism – something that is placed in the wrong historical time (e.g. a telescope in the hands of a Roman soldier)

analogy – a comparison that shows the resemblance between things in order to explain something clearly

antagonist – principal character in opposition to the protagonist or hero in fiction

chapter synopsis – an outline description saying briefly what is to happen in each chapter

cliffhanger – a nail-biting moment at the end of a chapter or just as the writer switches viewpoints

commission – this is when a publisher asks an author to write a book for them

dramatic irony – the reader knows something the characters don't; it could be scary!

editing – removing all unnecessary words from your story and getting it into the best shape possible

editor – the person who works in a publishing house and finds new books to publish. They also advise authors on how to improve their storytelling methods by telling them what needs adding or removing

first-person viewpoint – a viewpoint that allows a single character to tell the story as if they have written it. The reader feels as if that character is talking directly to them, e.g. 'It was July when I left for Timbuctoo. Just the thought of going back there made my heart sing'

foreshadowing – dropping hints of coming events or dangers that are essential to the outcome of the story

genre – a particular type of writing. 'Fantasy', 'historical', 'adventure' and 'science fiction' are all examples of different genres

historical fiction – fiction written in the present time about some past time

imagery – a way of describing something using 'word pictures'. See also 'metaphor' and 'simile'

internal critic – the voice that constantly picks holes in your work

light relief – a humorous scene used to give readers a rest from too much suspense, action or drama

list – the list of book titles that a publisher has already published or is about to publish

manuscript – your story when it is written down, either typed or by hand

metaphor – a way of describing something in a word picture. Calling a man 'a mouse' is a metaphor. It tells us that the man is timid or a coward, not that he actually *is* a mouse

motivation – the reason a character does something

narrative – the telling of the story or sometimes the story itself

omniscient viewpoint – an 'all-seeing' viewpoint that shows the reader the thoughts and feelings of all the characters

plagiarism – copying someone else's work and passing it off as your own. It is a serious offence

plot – the sequence of events that drives a story forwards; the problems that the hero must resolve

point of view (POV) – the eyes through which a story is told

primary source – the term historians use to describe first-hand accounts written in the historical period they are studying, e.g. letters, diaries or official documents like wills and marriage certificates

protagonist – the main character in a play or book

publisher – a person or company who pays for an author's manuscript to be printed as a book and who distributes and sells that book

rejection letter – the brief note that comes back from a publisher when they turn down your story

sequel – a story that carries an existing one forward

simile – a way of describing something by saying it is *like* something else, e.g. 'The clouds look like frayed lace'

slush pile – a term used by editors and publishers to describe all the unsolicited manuscripts that they receive every day from would-be writers

synopsis – a short summary that describes what a story is about and introduces the main characters

theme – the main idea behind your story, e.g. overcoming a weakness, the importance of friendship or good versus evil. A story can have more than one theme

third-person viewpoint – a viewpoint that describes the events of the story through a single character's eyes, e.g. 'Jem's heart leapt in his throat. Oh no! he thought. He'd been dreading this moment for months'

unsolicited submission – a manuscript that is sent to a publisher without them asking for it. These submissions usually end up in the 'slush pile'

writer's block – the feeling that writers get when they think they can no longer write, or have used up all their ideas

Most well-known writers have their own websites with information about their books. Many will give you hints and advice about writing, too.

Ask for a subscription to magazines such as *Cricket* and *Cicada*. They publish the best in young people's short fiction. See both magazines at www.cricketmag.com

Make a good friend of your local librarian. They will direct you to useful sources of information that you might not have thought of.

Ask your teacher to invite a favourite author to speak at your school. The Society of Authors website (www.societyofauthors.org) lists writers who visit schools.

Places to submit your historical fiction

• The magazine *Stone Soup* accepts stories and artwork from 8 to 13 year-olds. Their website is www.stonesoup.com

• The Young Writers Club is an Internet-based club where you can post your stories. Check it out at www.cs.bilkent.edu.tr/~david/derya/ywc.html

• *Potluck Children's Literary Magazine*: members.aol.com/potluckmagazine

Some historical sources

Look out for specialist magazines like *Archaeology* (www.archaeology.org) and *History Today* (www.historytoday.com).

For details of everyday life, the Costume Page (www.costumepage.org) has excellent links to sites that deal with dress through the ages.

For British history see www.bbc.co.uk/history and www.channel4.com/history
For American life in the 20th century see The Home Movie Archives at www.library.uml.edu/homemovies. For American history in general visit the Library of Congress American Memory Site at www.memory.loc.gov/ammem

Works quoted or mentioned in the text

Ghost Soldier, Elaine Marie Alphin, Henry Holt and Co.

Carrie's War, Nina Bawden, Puffin Modern Classics 2005

Code Talker; The Winter People, Joseph Bruchac, Dial 2005

Arthur – The Seeing Stone, Kevin Crossley-Holland, Orion 2003

Catherine, Called Birdy, Karen Cushman, HarperTrophy 2004

Great Expectations, Charles Dickens, 1861

A Northern Light/A Gathering Light, Jennifer Donnelly, Bloomsbury 2004

The Lady and the Squire, Terry Jones, Puffin 2000

The Enemies of Jupiter: The Roman Mysteries, Caroline Lawrence, Orion Children's Books 2003

Stop the Train, Geraldine McCaughrean, Oxford University Press 2001

Daughter of Venice, Donna Jo Napoli, Walker Books 2004

The Orphan Train Adventures, Joan Lowery Nixon, Random House

The Great Plague: The Diary of Alice Paynton London 1665–1666, Pamela Oldfield, Scholastic 2001

A Parcel of Patterns, Jill Paton Walsh, Puffin 1983

Riding the Flume, Patricia Curtis Pfitsch, Aladdin Paperbacks 2004

The Merry Adventures of Robin Hood, Howard Pyle, Signet Classics 1986

Witch Child, Celia Rees, Bloomsbury 2000

The House of Windjammer, V.A. Richardson, Bloomsbury 2004

Underground to Canada, Barbara Smucker, Puffin 1978

Roll of Thunder, Hear My Cry, Mildred D. Taylor, Puffin 1994

The Machine Gunners, Robert Westall, Macmillan 2001

Picture Credits: Art Archive: 8b, 32t, 35t, 46-47 all. Alamy: 40l. Corbis RF: 1, 3, 4, 13b, 14t, 18-19c, 40-41c, 41 all, 49r, 50t, 50b, 54t &c, 58-59 all, 62t. Creatas: 6t, 8t, 12t, 23t, 29br, 30t, 42t, 43 all, 48t, 56-57 all, Dickens House Museum: 10t, 16t. Getty images: 44-45c, 45t, 51t, 52-53c, 53t. Rex Features: 5 & 24, 6-7c, 8-9c, 9r, 11b, 18t, 20t, 22t, 22-23c, 26-27c, 28t, 28-29c, 30-31c, 32-33c, 33t, 34-35b, 36-37 all, 38-39 all, 42b, 42-43c, 44t, 50-51c, 54-55c, 55t & b, 60t. Werner Forman Archive: 7r, 11t, 12b, 13t, 14-15c, 16-17 all, 20-21c & r, 24t, 24c, 25t, 26t, 30b, 34t, 40b, 48b, 49t, 63b.